Breaking Controlling Powers

Breaking Controlling Powers

by
Roberts Liardon

Harrison House
Tulsa, Oklahoma

10th Printing
Over 90,000 in Print

Breaking Controlling Powers
(Revised)
ISBN 0-89274-887-7
(Formerly ISBN 0-89274-495-2)
Copyright © 1991 by Roberts Liardon
Roberts Liardon Ministries
P. O. Box 30710
Laguna Hills, California 92654

Contents

Breaking Controlling Powers

1

What Is Control?

Control seems to be a problem in every time of transition from an old wave of God's glory to a new wave, such as we are experiencing today. The power of control affects every circle of Christianity. The abuse of control holds people in unnecessary bondage and hinders them from fulfilling the purpose of God in their lives.

There is a *natural control* that people can exert over others, and there is a *self-control* that must be exercised within the individual. But there is also a *demonic control* that can be exercised by one person over another.

While this book will deal with the abuse of control, we will also examine the positive side of control, which is called "commitment." This God-given authority is placed on an individual who is committed to fulfill the plan of God in the earth and who looks to the Lord — not to people — for personal security and promotion.

Each of us needs to exercise self-control in order to keep ourselves free from sin. We exercise that control by applying the Word of God to our lives. The Word is the balance, and we must all use discipline in our daily experiences. But people who exercise abusive control seek to become the deciding factor in the lives of others. Such individuals replace the Word of God as the balance in the lives of those whom they dominate; they react negatively if they are not the control point of all decisions made.

We must realize that what is happening in the spiritual realm is being reflected in the natural realm. There is a great struggle going on in the world today for control of people's minds. This struggle is between the forces of light (Christianity) and the forces of darkness (Satanic powers).

Although Communism has deteriorated, the people of the world suffered enormously as a result of the ungodly natural control exercised by Communist control. Such totalitarian governments dominate people through fear, ignorance, and poverty, restricting their knowledge of the outside world and limiting their freedom of expression and religion.

As of this writing, I have traveled to some 40 nations of the world, including some that have been under and are still influenced by Communist rule, so I am writing from firsthand knowledge of the conditions that exist not only in the church world, but also in society in general.

In Communist states, I have lain in the back of a truck while live bullets rushed over my head. In these nations some people were killed because of their desire for political, economic, and religious freedom. I have seen the bread lines, and I have heard Christians in the underground churches voice the anguish of their lives.

However, people living in free societies are not immune to abusive control. This control may come from well-meaning parents, spouses, friends, creditors, spiritual leaders, even children. The purpose of this book is to help Christians recognize the core of the problem of abusive control and to understand its negative actions and reactions so they can be set free themselves and effectively minister to those who are still in bondage.

It is also important to recognize and understand the positive side of control in order to be able to accurately discern the difference between abusive and positive control, to submit to proper authority, and to grow into full maturity in the Body of Christ.

2

Abusive Control

Sometimes it is necessary to isolate, reveal, and understand the negative side of an issue in order to properly discern its positive side. In learning to operate in the realm of the spirit, we usually learn the correct methods of operation by trial and error. When we make a mistake, we correct it, make the proper adjustment, and go on.

Defining the problem is important because it helps to determine the solution. This is true in the area of abusive control.

Control does not originate in strangers. The devil does not use the beggar on the street to control the life of an individual Christian or the Church of Jesus Christ. Please understand that principle.

If a stranger walked into your home or down the aisle of your church, announcing that he had come on the premises to take over, you would throw him out. But if someone you know and trust were to come on the scene for the same purpose, you would not be so quick to eject him because of your personal respect for him.

At some point in the future, some of the people you respect right now may decide not to go on following the Lord. If you are not secure in the Lord yourself, this situation could cause a great problem in your life, your destiny, and your church. You must find your source of being in God and be able to discern accurately in the spirit.

9

Definition of Abusive Control

Let's begin our study by answering the question: What is abusive control?

Abusive control can be defined as "an attempt to dominate another person in order to fulfill one's own desires and to enhance personal security."

The individual who exercises abusive control has no personal regard or consideration for the one being controlled and dominated. The *abusive controller* may be a child, an adult, a spouse, a brother or sister, a parent or grandparent, an employee, a student, a church member, a leader, or a best friend. The controller's goal is survival, at any cost.

Characteristics of the Abusive Controller

An abusive controller is *insecure*. Although such a person may appear to handle everything with ease and confidence, inside he is scared, intimidated, and unfulfilled.

Fear of rejection is the motivating force behind the actions of an abusive controller. Although he may seem to be a person who can be depended upon, in truth he is the dependent one. Manipulation of others is important for him to feel needed, for that is his security.

Whenever we place our security in something or someone other than God, and God alone, we open ourselves to deception, defeat and despair. It is true that we need others to help encourage and sharpen us, but our dependency should be upon God, not people. We should never base our lives on the *opinions* of others around us. We should compare *people's words* with *God's words*, and follow the leading and direction of the Lord.

An abusive controller is *obsessed with supervising the behavior of others*. His entire focus is on someone or something other than himself. He cannot define the direction or describe the plan for his own life because he is so wrapped up in the person he is controlling. Whenever our security lies in something or someone other than God, it will fail.

An abusive controller *stifles the creative move of the Spirit through the person under his power*. Because he is bound by fear, he hinders the ability of others to be themselves. Many abusive controllers have a genuine desire to see the move of God operate accurately and successfully. But in attempting to promote that move, they can become religious and smother the true call and gifts of those around and under them. They usually avoid open expressions of feelings or direct, honest communication.

Because of his fear of rejection, an abusive controller has a *selfish personality*. He makes demands easily, and, many times, these demands are expressed ruthlessly.

An abusive controller has a *low sense of self-worth*. He has abandoned the problem within himself and has turned his entire focus on the problems of others. Fed by his sense of personal rejection, he bases his life and the result of it on what he can accomplish through his own works. He looks at those around him as his own accomplishments. If they fail, he feels that he is a failure himself.

Please understand that rejection has nothing to do with self-worth. Rejection is a strong, demonic spirit in the world. Whether we are accepted or rejected by others has nothing to do with our value or worth as children of God.

Nature of Abusive Control

Abusive control is an *illusion*. It is an imaginary sense of power used by the devil to deceive the one who wields it. No one can control the life and emotions of another. God Himself gave humankind a free will, and He will not violate our gift of choice and decision. The only person anyone can change and control is himself. God is not a God of illusion or fantasy; He is the God of reality.

11

Abusive control is *undermining* and, many times, *secretive*. It is accompanied by unnatural attachment, and every relationship it touches crumbles in destruction.

Finally, abusive control is characterized by *manipulation* — the main tool of the abusive controller who uses it to keep others in bondage to him. In the following two chapters we will discuss the primary areas of abusive control: emotional and spiritual manipulation.

3
Emotional Manipulation

However we may evaluate abusive control, it still finds its source in a reactionary process. An abusive controller will either *overreact* or *underreact* — whichever it takes to keep his victim suspended. This happens because an abusive controller finds fulfillment in the *soulish realm.*

The soulish realm produces a false sense of security, giving ground to the work of demonic spirits. Instead of finding and fulfilling his rightful place of commitment and security in Christ Jesus, an abusive controller attempts to pamper himself and others through the use of personal power and unnatural respect.

Types of Emotional Manipulation

The principal method used by an abusive controller is *emotional manipulation.* Tears and helplessness, anger, threats, and silence are all primary instruments of emotional manipulation. Silence, which is a form of rejection, is an especially powerful emotional tool.

Many people become controlled by their own emotions because they make their decisions primarily based on *feelings.* This is precisely why they make so many wrong decisions!

In fact, the mistake of many Christians is making their decisions on feelings rather than on the leadership of the Holy Spirit. Finding security in Jesus will be the deciding factor between feelings and accurate direction by the Holy Spirit.

This is the primary reason many young people end up choosing the wrong marriage partner, leading to unhappiness and, often, divorce.

This is why some career people end up making wrong business decisions, losing everything they own.

This is why many a servant of God is filling the wrong pulpit. (Just because a congregation is nice to a minister does not mean that he is called to become their pastor!)

Tears and Helplessness

A classic example of emotional manipulation starts when both sets of parents want a recently married couple to spend the Christmas holidays with them.

It begins innocently enough when the bride mentions to her mother, "I think we are going to John's parents' for Christmas." The mother starts crying and complaining, "You don't love us anymore, or you would come to our house for the holidays!"

This negative reaction throws the daughter into an emotional state. She wavers and finally agrees to change their plans.

But when the bridegroom calls his mother with the news, she is equally upset and adamant. "But we have everything all planned!" she wails. "We can't possibly change things now!"

Many people are controlled through such displays of emotion. It happens not only to newlyweds but to people in every stage of life.

Often, when someone doesn't agree with the controlling person, he will start whining, "You don't love me," or, "You don't want me around anymore."

Not all abusive controllers rule with an iron hand. Some come clothed in sweetness and gentleness. These particular controllers are lethal. If they can't manifest a tear, they will sometimes revert to helplessness. Their intention is to make their victim feel an overwhelming sense of responsibility to them and to their lives.

Such controllers know how to play on the strings of guilt and pity. They control through their supposed sickness, weakness, and victimization. Although sometimes their ailments or infirmities are legitimate, more often they are fabricated or at least exaggerated. These people make their victims feel that if they are not pampered and petted, their whole world will crumble.

Do you know what you should do if you find yourself being exploited by this type of abusive controller? Be gentle but firm. Let that person know that you are not going to allow yourself to be emotionally manipulated.

If someone tries to make you feel obligated to change your long-established plans just to suit his or her selfish desires, say, "My feelings for you have nothing to do with the circumstances. I am sorry that you are upset, but this is just the way things are."

If you are being misused and abused by a sympathy-seeking exploiter, just tell him or her, "I don't like it when you act this way. You are missing the point of my responsibilities."

Sometimes you may have to be blunt and say, "I don't have to agree with you in this area and be manipulated by your attitude."

Don't fall into the trap of emotional manipulation by thinking that something is wrong with you. Judge yourself by the Word of God. If you have peace within, then know that the emotional outburst of the other person is an indication of his or her *problem* or *present circumstance* and not a reflection on you.

Anger

If a display of tears and helplessness won't work, often a controlling person will retreat into anger — and most people do not know how to handle an individual who is angry.

Do you know what to do with an angry person? Just stay calm. Do not react. By your overreacting, an entire chain of negative events could be set off. Don't do anything that might provoke or justify improper behavior.

Just look at the angry person, state the truth calmly and quietly, and refuse to react negatively! By refusing to react to anger, you remove yourself from the power of this type of abusive control.

Learn to stop reacting in ways that are not necessary and do not work. Sometimes it is good to leave an angry person alone with his rage.

An angry individual may not know what to do in that situation. He may hit the wall and beat on the chair. If he does, when you come back into the room simply say to him, "Why did you punch a hole in my wall? Is that the action of an adult?"

Understand that when you disarm an abusive controller, extreme emotions will surface. Anger will monopolize the atmosphere, as well as your thoughts, if you are not careful. Angry words will hit your mind like machine gun bullets, preventing you from defending yourself properly.

Keep your perspective clear and precise. When you make the choice to live responsibly, others must live that way also.

Threats

Words of failure, defeat, unnatural obligation, guilt, criticism, and intimidation often follow. These threats are all used in an attempt to control a person's life. They are designed to paralyze with fear, and to produce the result the abusive controller is seeking.

The Bible has much to say about the power of words:

> **Death and life are in the power of the tongue: and they that love it shall eat the fruit thereof.**
>
> **Proverbs 18:21**

Scripture refers to words as "swords" (Ps. 59:7; Heb. 4:12; Rev. 1:16; 19:15), and those spoken negatively in our lives will have an adverse effect if we receive them and live according to them.

The Amplified Bible version of Psalm 55:21 says:

> **The words of his mouth were smoother than cream or butter, but war was in his heart; his words were softer than oil, yet they were drawn swords.**

Again *The Amplified Bible* has this interpretation of Psalm 59:7:

> **Behold, they belch out [insults] with their mouth; swords [of sarcasm, ridicule, slander, and lies] are in their lips; for who, they think, hears us?**

Just as a sword or an arrow pierces the heart on a battlefield, so negative words are designed to pierce the heart of the hearer. If words are spoken negatively and abusively, they will wound and hurt deeply if not removed. No one can carry negative words in his heart and still fulfill the plan and purpose of God for his life, just as he cannot walk around with a sword or an arrow thrust in his chest and live long!

Here is an example of threatening words. Suppose you announce in full assurance that God has called you to leave home and loved ones behind and to go serve Him in a far-off place. An abusive controller will reply by saying, "You'll never make it there," or, "You'll probably die there." Sometimes he or she will threaten your relationship by responding, "If you go, don't ever contact me again," or,

"If you go, you will not be welcome in this house anymore." Even financial threats may be used: "If you go, I will not send you any more money," or, "If you go, you will go broke and starve."

Such words are an attack against you! Words of failure and defeat dominate the lives of many people without their even being aware of it.

How do you "pull" these negative, abusive words out of your heart? By counterattacking them with the Word of God. The first half of Hebrews 4:12 (AMP) tells us:

For the Word that God speaks is alive and full of power — making it active, operative, energizing and effective; it is sharper than any two-edged sword....

Speak the Word of God over yourself. Scripture says that the Word of God is sharper than any other "sword." The accurate Word will calm and heal the wounds of abusive words. Negative words can affect your life only if you allow them to do so.

Silence

If tears, anger and threats will not work, then the controlling person will attempt to use silence as a weapon. He will shut out his victim by ignoring him and keeping him dangling, wondering what the controller is thinking and how he is feeling.

Those who are weak in spirit cannot handle such treatment. That is why weak people are so easily controlled.

If someone is trying to control you by use of silence, what should you do? Nothing! Let that individual be silent! Go on with your business and your life. Don't let silence control your activities and make you nervous. Don't get into turmoil because of what someone else is doing or not doing. Make a choice to live in joy and contentment.

Sometimes in a church, an elder or a deacon will resort to this kind of manipulation against the pastor. If this happens, the pastor should confront the issue. If the controlling person will not respond, repent, and change, the pastor should remove him from the board until he shows evidence of spiritual growth and maturity.

Avoid Dependence on Another

Do not be overly dependent on other people. Do not expect others to pray on your behalf and get answers from heaven for you. It doesn't matter how spiritual you think they are, or how accurate others have been in the past. Godly counsel is good, but if you direct your life and future from the word of another, you are setting yourself up for control and misery.

You must hear from God for yourself, then *mature it* from the godly counsel of others who have proven themselves. God has a plan for your life. He may *mature* that plan through others, but He will not *lead you* through another.

Fear will cause you to depend upon another person. The Bible says that the Holy Spirit is our Guide. He will lead from within.

If you are a dependent person, you cannot enjoy normal fellowship with others, because your joy, happiness, and thoughts will come from them — not from the real you.

4
Spiritual Manipulation

In discussing abusive control, it must be noted that the area of spiritual manipulation is by far the most dangerous. It is dangerous for both the controller and the one being controlled because it treads on the spiritual principles of heaven.

Like emotional manipulation, spiritual manipulation is based on the soulish realm. It has *nothing* to do with *the true spiritual realm*. It is still *soulish maneuvering*, but it uses a spiritual principle as its primary tool.

By recalling the attributes of an abusive controller, we can see many reasons why such a person would revert to spiritual manipulation.

If an individual cannot control another person through emotions, he will refer to a "higher power" — a form of spiritual manipulation — to keep his victim subservient to him.

Spiritual manipulators are those who have not developed godly character in a particular area. They are led by their lust or desire for control, rather than by the Spirit of God.

In First Timothy 3:2,6 we read these words:

A bishop then must be blameless....

Not a novice, *lest being lifted up with pride* he fall into the condemnation of the devil.

One of the reasons the Apostle Paul wrote this passage was to warn Timothy against allowing a young, inexperienced convert to assume the responsibilities of spiritual leadership. Paul knew the danger of promoting too quickly those who are not yet spiritually mature. Such people often fall prey to the temptation of pride. They tend to get "puffed up" if they are given a high position in the church. Instead of humbly serving the Body of Christ, they become pious and manipulative.

Then there are those upon whom God has truly bestowed a special anointing or gift. Again, if they have not fully matured, often such people will feel that they are among the elite and will carry about them an air of superiority. They will look down on others whom they consider "less spiritual" than they are and will often use or abuse those under their authority rather than loving and caring for them.

Such people fail to recognize that a strong, godly character helps their gift or anointing to operate at its full potential and to last a lifetime. Those who don't concentrate on building a strong character may lose what gift and anointing they have been given.

God has no "superstars"; He only has servants. If a servant does his job, God will promote him. But no matter how great his name may become, a true servant will still have a desire to meet the needs of the people in his charge and to help them when they are in trouble. That is what a ministry gift is for. The true servant must be careful not to use his God-given authority to "lord it over" others.

God is a personal God Who speaks to the hearts of men and women individually. Believers who are in leadership roles must be particularly careful to say exactly what the Lord tells them to say — nothing more and nothing less! Leaders have a responsibility to make certain that when they say that something is of God, it really is. They do this by spending time in prayer, by searching the Scriptures, and by seeking seasoned, godly counsel.

Control by the "Superspiritual"

It never fails; in every church there are members who think everyone should obey them because they have been there the longest or because they are the most spiritual. Either such people will seek to dominate the leadership in every decision made or they will give their advice on every personal circumstance among the members.

Do not base your life on the opinions of another person, especially if that individual has not been ordained by God for leadership. Line up every statement you hear against the Word of God. According to Romans 8:16, we will know the voice of the Lord by our inner witness, not by the soulish feelings or opinions of others.

These "superspiritual" people watch for those over whom they can exercise spiritual manipulation. If you have a spiritual call upon your life, they will recognize it and will single you out for their "special ministry." Many times such "superspiritual" people are unseasoned themselves, so they will give you "words from the Lord" that will push you out ahead of God's perfect timing. If you are led more strongly by ambition than by the Spirit of God, you will fall for such illusions. Many genuine calls upon people's lives have been aborted because of "superspiritual" abusive controllers.

How do these people abort calls? There are several ways.

One is by organizing a Bible study with someone other than the pastor as leader because "the pastor does not teach the *deep* things of the Spirit." Not only does this spell trouble (especially if you are the one chosen to lead this special "Bible study"), this kind of behavior is also the core for a church split.

Don't fall prey to this type of spiritual delusion. If it is time for you to be in a position of leadership, God will put you on the field or He will motivate the pastor to invite you to lead a segment of the Body — under his supervision. Take the time of your training very seriously, and do not allow yourself to be pushed out ahead of God's timetable by an ambitious controller who wants to take the credit for your success.

Another way abusive controllers abort calls is by giving out false "words from the Lord" or false "visions." Usually such words or visions are either extremely morbid or extremely favorable. They are designed for the same purpose: to push the hearer out ahead of God's timing and ultimately to abort the call of God upon his life.

The truth is, people who give out such words and visions have not had a visitation from God. Beware of giving heed to such self-styled "prophets." When it comes to your personal call, why would God speak something to someone else that He has not already shared with you? Personal prophecies and visions concerning another person are to be a *confirmation* of what the individual already knows in his heart. If another person can entirely lead your life through prophecies and visions, you will never be a leader for God.

The Word of God is very strong against false prophecies and visions. The prophet Jeremiah faced this same kind of situation in his day and cut through the deceit of the religious controllers. (Jer. 23.)

In essence he said to them, "You people prophesy out of *your own hearts*. You say that you have received a vision from the Lord when in reality it was just in *your own heads*. You are telling people that there is going to be peace, when there is really going to be war. And you are assuring them that they are fine, when they are actually guilty of worshipping themselves.

"You are prophesying falsely. You are speaking out of your own hearts, rather than out of the heart of heaven.

To you the Lord says, 'I am against you, and you shall be judged.'"

Do not fall into the trap of receiving false "words" or "visions." To be a leader who follows God, you must know the Lord for yourself and exercise His character in order to hear His plan for your life and to follow His perfect timing.

The devil wants to destroy your calling and thwart your purpose in the earth. His plan of attack will be based on your weaknesses. He will attempt to execute that plan in the way that you least expect, and he will succeed unless you are sensitive to the Spirit of God.

One final way abusive controllers try to abort divine calls is by acting very spiritual. They *act as though* they are spiritual people, but in reality their control is of the devil.

Controlling Prayers

Another variation of spiritual manipulation is *controlling prayers*. Can Christians pray controlling prayers? Certainly they can! But if misused, these prayers are a form of witchcraft!

As we have studied in Chapter 2, the Bible says that our words are like "swords" and that they contain power.

Remember: *Words are spiritual weapons.*

A *controlling prayer* is composed of words with a spiritual force behind them, spoken to influence the course of another's life. The only time a controlling prayer should be used by a Christian is when the Word and the Spirit of God are used to come against the enemy. Jesus explained this method of prayer in binding and loosing the plan of God against the devil's will. (Matt. 16:19.)

An abusive controller prays *his own human desires or will for someone else out of his own human heart*. He is trying to make the other individual obey his selfish desires rather than the Lord's will for that person's life.

The person praying may or may not understand that he is loosing evil influences in the spirit realm. A controlling prayer is harmful and misused when it violates or dominates another person's *will*. Then it becomes a form of witchcraft.

In other words, through prayer in the spirit realm an abusive controller looses demonic influence to control the natural life of another person for the controller's own benefit.

In Matthew, Chapter 12, Jesus had just healed a man possessed with a blind and mute evil spirit. The people started to murmur among themselves for they could not believe the miracle they had just witnessed. In response, Jesus began to teach them about the power of words. In verse 37 (AMP) of that passage He said to them:

For by your words you will be justified and acquitted, and by your words you will be condemned and sentenced.

With our words we can bless or curse. Controlling prayer falls under the category of a curse, because they are words spoken against another person in an attempt to satisfy selfish human desires.

An example of a controlling prayer is the one prayed by a mother who does not approve of the girl some young man is dating. She wants him to marry her daughter instead, so she prays that the romance will fail and that he will choose her daughter as his bride.

I know of a particular case very much like this. A mother prayed and prayed that a young married couple would get a divorce so the husband would "see the light" and marry her daughter. Because of this mother's unceasing *soulish* prayers, trouble was sent into this marriage *by her words*. Finally the couple became aware of the situation. They rose up and broke the power of the words spoken against them in the spirit realm, and their marriage continued to prosper.

Soulish prayers can occur in any area of life where human desire is placed *over* the will of God.

One of the most commonly *misquoted* scriptures in the Bible, often used with soulish prayers, is Psalm 37:4, which reads:

Delight thyself also in the Lord; and he shall give thee the desires of thine heart.

I cannot count how many times I have heard this verse quoted by Christians who have placed their own desires *over* the will of God for their lives — and expected to have those selfish desires fulfilled.

In examining this verse in its true context, we will see an interesting aspect of it which is totally different from the way it is usually interpreted by most believers.

In Strong's concordance, we see that the meaning of the Hebrew word translated *delight* in this passage is "to be *soft* or pliable."[1]

The point the psalmist is making in this passage is that when a person "delights" himself in the Lord, he allows God to *reform* his heart, making it soft and pliable to His will and His purpose.

If we truly delight ourselves in the Lord, then our wills are transformed so that it is *His* desire we seek and not *our own*.

When we fully and completely delight ourselves in God, our soulish desires *must change*, and our hearts become united with His heart. Once we are in that place of softness and submission, we learn to trust Him totally in every area of our lives.

So here in Psalm 37:4 the psalmist is speaking of a complete "heart transplant," in which we turn *our will* over

---

[1]James Strong, *The Exhaustive Concordance of the Bible* (Nashville: Abingdon, 1890) "Hebrew and Chaldee Dictionary," p. 89, #6026.

to the Lord, seeking *His will* and *trusting Him* to lead us in the way that He wants us to go. Our desire becomes His desire — and then we are promised that we shall have the (godly) desire of our heart.

Spiritual manipulators twist scriptures to give substance to their controlling prayers. They do not have the heart of God in any situation. *They* want to be God and to make *their* plans work. Spiritual controllers think they know what is best for everyone involved. Since they do not have the heart of God, they cannot know the will of God.

Don't Fear Them

Although soulish, controlling prayers can trouble our lives, we do not need to fear them or become paranoid about them. We only need to be aware of them. They cannot succeed in lives that are *totally* committed to God.

The only prayers that are effective, according to the Word of God, are *fervent prayers*. It is impossible for a controlling prayer to be truly fervent.

The word *fervent* does not mean "desperate," nor does it means "intense" or "unceasing."

In James 5:16 we read these words:

> . . . The effectual *fervent* prayer of a righteous man availeth much.

Years ago, the Lord took me to this verse and caused the word *fervent* to stand out to me. I asked myself what it meant to be fervent.

As I began to study this verse, I came to Matthew 12:25 which helped me understand why a fervent prayer prevails with God:

> And Jesus knew their thoughts, and said unto them, Every kingdom divided against itself is brought to desolation; and every city or house divided against itself shall not stand.

We, as individuals, are a "kingdom" made up of three parts: a spirit, a soul, and a body. Therefore, you are not *just* a mind or a desire; you are a *spirit* that owns a *mind* and lives in a *body.*

Your mind and your body are pieces of "equipment" that are needed in order for your spirit to carry out the purpose of God in the earth.

If you do not properly understand the "equipment" you have been given, you cannot pray effectively.

In prayer, God does not talk to a piece of your "equipment" — the mind! The Lord speaks to your heart — your spirit man — the *real* you. The plans of heaven come to you through your spirit. That is how God will communicate with you. Your mind may find out a few seconds later and be able to interpret what your spirit has received. That is why your spirit sometimes knows something, but you are not able to put it into words because your mind has not yet comprehended it.

If the three parts of your "kingdom" are divided, you will not be able to pray effectively, and you will fail. If your spirit is not leading, you are divided.

In fervent prayer your spirit, soul, and body go together into the arena of prayer and worship.

Your spirit, soul, and body are as one, united in the purpose of God to see His plan fulfilled, His will done. Your spirit is your source of prayer, and your soul (desires, emotions, imaginations, memories) and body (actions) work together and are submitted to it.

A person who prays controlling prayers is not "together." No matter how spiritual he may act, if he prays from his desire rather than from his spirit, he will not succeed. Spiritual manipulators move strongly in the soulish realm, and they will reap a soulish result.

A spiritual controller faces three different directions. He can go by the body way, or the head way, but he usually avoids the spirit way, because it involves a cost — total subjection of personal will to the will of God.

Controlling prayers are born from worry, frustration, and flesh. The Bible indicates that because desire, and not the spirit, is the core of their thrust, such prayers represent a house divided and will fail.

In Proverbs 26:2 we are told:

> **As the bird by wandering, as the swallow by flying, so the curse *causeless* shall not come.**

Again, in Strong's concordance we see that the Hebrew word translated *causeless* means "devoid of cost."[2]

As a strong believer, you need not be concerned about controlling prayers if you are following the will of God and fulfilling His purpose, seasoning yourself in the Word and developing in godly character. The Bible indicates that if your heart has taken on the will of God for your life, you are "paying the price." Proverbs 26:2 says that any words spoken against you by someone who has not "paid the price" (borne the cost) to know God and His ways and character will not destroy you.

As a believer, you can prevail against any soulish prayers that hinder you. Put the Word of God into practice in your life. Develop a strong sensitivity to the Holy Spirit and His timings in every area. Be committed to godly character and bold integrity. These principles produce security in Him and enable you to follow as *He* leads you.

Control by Spiritual Gifts

Unfortunately, some can even misuse their gifts in a public setting to control others.

---

[2]James Strong, *The Exhaustive Concordance of the Bible* (Nashville: Abingdon, 1890), "Hebrew and Chaldee Dictionary," p. 41, #2600.

Suppose you are in a lively Gospel meeting. Everyone is rejoicing and shouting and praising God. All of a sudden, someone raises his hands and yells, "Thus saith the Lord." He then delivers a supposed prophecy. (Read First Corinthians, Chapter 14, for a detailed study of the proper functioning of the gifts of the Spirit in public gatherings.)

In every Gospel meeting, there are all sorts of people present, and each one operates from a different level of spiritual maturity. We must learn to mature ourselves in the spirit and hear the voice of the Lord accurately. We must not accept an operation of the spirit just because the majority of the people seem to be ecstatic about it. Do not follow the *mood* of the people; follow the *move* of the Holy Spirit.

After the person has given the prophecy, everyone in the meeting screams, "Yes!" But your spirit says, "No!" If you are not strong in the spirit, you may be swayed by such "hyperflesh" moves and prophecies.

Why would the majority accept such a prophecy as from the Lord?

One of the reasons is that some have been mesmerized by spiritual gifts instead of being influenced by godly character. Some people become so awed by an exciting display that they do not stop to discern what is true and what is false. They do not realize that Jesus taught that we will know the servants of God by their *fruits*, not by their *gifts*. (Matt. 7:20.)

We do not discount the gifts of God in any way, for they are priceless to the Body of Christ. However, we must mature in the realm of the Spirit. We must understand the *character* of God so we can know when the gifts are in *true operation*.

One of the attributes of the Holy Spirit is that He will always exalt Jesus — *not another human being.*

I have been in meetings in which the eyes of the people were called continually to focus on "the man of God" and how "*he* would heal" and "*he* would bring deliverance." It is a sad fact, but some people are ready to follow anyone or anything that appears "spiritual." Only God will heal and bring deliverance; and while it is true that He may use humankind to reveal Himself through, *He alone* must receive all the glory, praise, and honor.

The flesh attempts to control the moves of God. Many of the things that people label "spiritual" actually come from the mental realm. You will know whether something is of God or not by discerning whether it points toward or away from self. If someone has a "revelation" — or even a prophecy — that benefits, exalts, or glorifies self, then it is not of God.

The security of the flesh is always centered in another person — another self — not in God. *Find your security in God so you will be motivated by commitment rather than by control.*

5
Abusive Control in the Bible

Now let's examine the problem of abusive control from a biblical perspective. Let's see how Jesus managed to remove Himself from people who sought to abusively control Him:

> And when the devil had ended all the temptation, he departed from him for a season.

> And Jesus returned in the power of the Spirit into Galilee: and there went out a fame of him through all the region round about.

> And he taught in their synagogues, being glorified of all.

> And he came to Nazareth, where he had been brought up: and, as his custom was, he went into the synagogue on the sabbath day, and stood up for to read.

> And there was delivered unto him the book of the prophet Esaias. And when he had opened the book, he found the place where it was written,

> The Spirit of the Lord is upon me, because he hath anointed me to preach the gospel to the poor; he hath sent me to heal the brokenhearted, to preach deliverance to the captives, and recovering of sight to the blind, to set at liberty them that are bruised.

> To preach the acceptable year of the Lord.

> And he closed the book, and he gave it again to the minister, and sat down. And the eyes of all them that were in the synagogue were fastened on him.

> And he began to say unto them, This day is this
> scripture fulfilled in your ears.
>
> Luke 4:13-21

This is an interesting story. Jesus knew His destiny. He knew His call to the earth. But He didn't advertise it before it was time; He kept it to Himself and developed it.

Jesus went through His wilderness experience and *won*. (Luke 4:1-12.) Most people go into their wilderness and *stay* there. They do not get very far when faced with trials and temptation. The first time the devil tells them they can't succeed, they agree. "That's right," they say, and sit down in defeat and despair. God, however, is looking for fighters, not weak-kneed, wishy-washy Christians. The world has seen enough of those people.

After Jesus had emerged victorious from His wilderness experience, He walked back to His hometown, Nazareth, where He had grown up, and entered the synagogue.

This was where His parents had "gone to church." It was where the minister had trained Him as a boy. Jesus had learned many good things from the leader of that synagogue.

That day, when the pastor handed the scrolls to Jesus, He opened them and read Isaiah 61:1,2. But Jesus did not read this prophecy as a normal man would read it — as something the people expected to take place in the future. *Jesus read the prophetic message as if it applied to Him — because it did!*

Control in the Home Church

After Jesus had boldly announced, ...**This day is this scripture** [prophecy] **fulfilled in your ears** (Luke 4:21), the people's first reaction was, ...**Is not this Joseph's son?** (v. 22).

*The people of Nazareth totally missed the significance of Jesus'
declaration that He was the Messiah!* All they could say was,
"No, You can't be; You're the son of Joseph, the local
carpenter."

*As Jesus spoke further, calling Himself a prophet, the people
became incensed.* (vv. 23-27.)

> **And all they in the synagogue, when they heard
> these things, were filled with wrath.**
>
> **And rose up, and thrust him out of the city, and
> led him unto the brow of the hill whereon their city
> was built, that they might cast him down headlong.**
>
> **But he passing through the midst of them went
> his way.**
>
> **Luke 4:28-30**

*When you take possession of what is yours spiritually, people
who are lukewarm will automatically oppose you!* A lukewarm
person is double minded. He "sits on the fence" between
listening to his emotions or his spirit.

Jesus closed the book and handed it back to the
minister. He did the right and respectful thing. He had read
forcefully from the scriptures in the Spirit, but He did not
try to take over the meeting. He sat down.

If Looks Could Kill . . .

The people of Nazareth were so astonished at Jesus that
they did not simply glance at Him; their eyes were fastened
on Him, as we saw in verse 20. After He had spoken to them
strongly about their lack of faith in Him as the promised
Messiah (vv. 23-27), their look became warlike: a look of
madness, a look of rage, a look beyond natural
understanding — a look that demands to know, "Who do
You think You are?" (v. 28.)

Has anyone ever looked at you that way? If you are
a true servant of God, you may undergo this type of
persecution.

35

Notice that Jesus did not respond to their anger — and because He didn't, they wanted to destroy Him!

This was Jesus, the young man who had grown up in their "church." This was Nazareth, one of those small towns where everyone knows everyone else's business! And everyone supposedly loves everyone else. But not now.

The people in Nazareth wanted to kill Jesus because He did not withdraw, explain, or falter. He stood His ground.

They could not control Him! He was not under their power!

When you get to the place where people can't control you through intimidation or other means, they may try to destroy you. They may cast you out. In other words, they may try to excommunicate you.

The people of Nazareth rose up as one to run Jesus out of town and throw Him off a nearby hilltop. (v. 29.) This was a dramatic excommunication: They wanted to kill Him!

They were looking for God's Anointed One, and they thought they would recognize Him through their usual carnal ways of thinking. But they failed to recognize the Messiah when He came and lived in their midst as one of them! Even after all the teachings He had delivered and all the miracles He had preformed among them, they still did not believe that Jesus was the Messiah! Why? Because they had been blinded by *religion*.

What is *religion*? It is an attempt to know and please God through human effort. *Christianity* is not a religion; it is a relationship with God — walking side by side, talking and communicating with Jesus, the Living Son of God. This personal relationship does not come through religion, in which people seek to know and please God through human artifacts and personal opinions.

This is why there are "religious spirits" — demons sent to bind people from knowing God personally in His fullness. Religious spirits are controlling spirits. They insist on fleshly operations and manifestations to make people feel that they have done a service to God. Religious, controlling spirits hinder the true move of the Spirit of God. They operate through those who walk by the flesh, those who do not know much about life in the Spirit. Such people are very unlearned about a spiritual relationship with Jesus Christ; however, they know all the "religious" facts, and usually distort them to control the move of the Holy Spirit.

Notice that in this passage Jesus did not die. He just walked through the midst of that angry crowd and went on His way. He had a destiny to fulfill; humankind could not control Him or abort His mission.

Even the ones whom Jesus loved most could not control Him or hinder what God had called Him to do.

This is an example of a controlling spirit which operated through Jesus' "home church" in an effort to make Him back down from saying that He, the Messiah, had come into the world to fulfill the prophetic scriptures.

The Early Church Faces Control

Now let's turn to the fourth chapter of Acts, where we will see an example of attempted control in the early Church. We will see how the religious leaders of Israel attempted to control the Apostles Peter and John after the lame man at the Gate Beautiful had been healed through them by the power of Jesus' name:

And as they [Peter and John] spake unto the people, the priests, and the captain of the temple, and the Sadducees, came upon them,

Being grieved that they taught the people, and preached through Jesus the resurrection from the dead.

And laid hands on them, and put them in hold unto the next day: for it was now eventide....

And it came to pass on the morrow, that their rulers, and elders, and scribes,

And Annas the high priest, and Caiaphas, and John, and Alexander, and as many as were of the kindred of the high priest, were gathered together at Jerusalem.

And when they had set them in the midst, they asked, By what power, or by what name, have ye done this?

Then Peter, filled with the Holy Ghost, said unto them, Ye rulers of the people, and elders of Israel,

If we this day be examined of the good deed done to the impotent man, by what means he is made whole;

Be it known unto you all [not just some of you; *all* of you], and to all the people of Israel, that by the name of Jesus Christ of Nazareth, whom ye crucified, whom God raised from the dead, even by him doth this man stand here before you whole.

Acts 4:1-3,5-10

That was a bold statement. Here, all the religious spirits in town had come together to attack Peter and John for healing a sick man! This tells us that religious spirits are not on the side of God, because no one should be angry when a sick person is healed. Instead, there should be rejoicing!

Have you noticed from this scripture passage that people who are "religious" have no common sense? They think they are on fire for God, but in reality they are very cold spiritually. When someone tells them that they are cold spiritually, or when God uses someone outside of their control system, they become very angry!

Controlling People and Religious People

There is really no way to separate controlling people from religious people. Controlling spirits and religious spirits are alike. They are identical twins — it is hard to have one without the other. You will find many controllers among those who are very religious.

But notice that Peter was not afraid to respond to strong religious people. One way to stand up to controlling, religious spirits is never to fear them and to always have a spiritual response ready to give to them. Also notice that when abusive controllers began to attack God's servants, a response to them was always recorded in the Bible.

Why were the religious leaders of Jerusalem attacking the apostles? To stop them from healing the people in the name of Jesus. The leaders were afraid that the healings would affect their control over people whom they thought they "owned."

Peter, being full of the Holy Spirit, explained to all of these religious leaders that healing people is a "good deed" (v. 9), not a wicked or mischievous deed.

When confronting controlling people, you need to state the truth. Don't just suggest it, state it. That's what Peter did. He went on to tell the leaders that the healing had come about ...**by the name of Jesus Christ of Nazareth, whom ye crucified**...(v. 10). That is another bold statement!

Peter was addressing the same leaders who had allowed a murderer to go free in order to have Jesus crucified. Peter's bold statements didn't make these controlling, religious people very happy. They marvelled at the apostles, but they also made degrading statements about them:

> **Now when they saw the boldness of Peter and John, and perceived that they were unlearned and ignorant men, they marvelled; and they took knowledge of them, that they had been with Jesus.**

39

> And beholding the man which was healed standing with them, they could say nothing against it.

> But when they had commanded them [which is characteristic of controllers; they don't ask, they command. There is always an undercurrent of demand in their statements, causing the other person to feel obligated to comply with their desires] to go aside out of the council, they conferred among themselves.

> Saying, What shall we do to these men? for that indeed a notable miracle hath been done by them is manifest to all them that dwell in Jerusalem; and we cannot deny it.

> But that it spread no further among the people, let us straitly *threaten* them, that they speak henceforth to no man in this name.

> And they called them, and *commanded* them not to speak at all nor teach in the name of Jesus.

> Acts 4:13-18

Biblical Threats

We have discussed the abusive threats that can manifest in daily living. But now, let's see the biblical threats that the men of God had to deal with in the Scriptures.

Notice the phrase in verse 17, . . . **let us straitly** *threaten* **them**. . . . What does a threat do to a person? It makes him go against what he believes; it forces him to submit to those who are intimidating him. That is abusive control!

The religious leaders of that day threatened the apostles by commanding . . . **them not to speak at all nor teach in name of Jesus** (v. 18). That was control, and the apostles had a decision to make in response to it.

How did Peter and John react in the face of these threats and demands?

> But Peter and John answered and said unto them, Whether it be right in the sight of God to hearken unto you more than unto God, judge ye.

For we cannot but speak the things which we have seen and heard.

So when they had *further threatened them*, they let them go, finding nothing how they might punish them, because of the people: for all men glorified God for that which was done.

Acts 4:19-21

I like these apostles! They stood their ground before all the religious spirits in town. The religious leaders were angry because a miracle had been done — and because it hadn't been done through them! They thought *they* should have been the ones to perform the miracle, because they were the religious rulers. However, God could not use them, because they were full of pride, thinking they knew it all.

God is not looking for a person who operates from his head — by his own way of thinking. God is looking for someone who operates from his heart — by his spirit. God is looking for human beings who will be obedient to His Spirit.

That is why it bothers some well-educated, prideful people when God uses someone who has little or no formal education to be a miracle-worker.

People who are filled with pride usually criticize those who have nothing in the natural. But how can God use those who are relying on their education alone? *The only way an education works for a person is by submitting it to the will of God and not relying upon it, but solely upon God!*

In the seventh verse of this passage, these religious leaders asked the apostles, . . . **By what power, or by what name, have ye done this?** They were saying, "Who do you think you are, doing such a thing without *our* permission? By whose authority did you do this?"

41

Biblical Defeat of Control

The eighth verse continues, **Then Peter, filled with the Holy Ghost, said unto them....**

The only way to win over control is to be full of the Holy Spirit and power! Just like Peter, we need the Spirit of Might in order to win over the spirits of control.

Though it is important to speak words of faith and not of doubt, the Spirit of Might (Is. 11:2) does not come upon a person as a result of his reciting positive confessions or following prescribed formulas. It will not *stay* on an individual just because he associates with the "right people."

The Spirit of Might places a passion within the believer that will motivate him to hate evil and will empower him to carry out God's plan in the earth. The Spirit of Might is as a nuclear force resident within the individual that propels him forward over every evil opponent that may attempt to restrain him.

The Spirit of Might confronts resistance. It provides the individual the ability to distinguish right from wrong in any situation, and to go on from there. It never defends; it simply endows the person it indwells with the power to state the facts!

The Spirit of Might gives the human mind the supernatural ability to remain in peace and to rest in the midst of battle. It brings the assurance of the coming victory and causes the joy of the Lord to manifest around the one who possesses it.

The Spirit of Might also endows the physical body and the emotions with endurance and protection. It supplies the supernatural ability to carry on far beyond the natural, soulish limitations.

The Spirit of Might never comes upon a person for the purpose of self-gain. It comes in order that the purpose of God may be fulfilled in the earth through the Church!

Peter had the Spirit of Might in and upon him as he spoke in the face of the religious leaders of his day. In verse 10, he continued his discourse by telling them, "By the name of Jesus Christ of Nazareth — Whom you crucified — that's by Whose name we performed this miracle, and by Whose name we will continue to perform miracles!"

The religious leaders responded by commanding the apostles to stop teaching and preaching in this name, threatening them severely if they did not obey.

But what did Peter and John do? They went back to their own company and told everyone of the things that had happened. (v. 23.)

Did the Church in the book of Acts shrink back because of the report they received from the apostles? No! The Spirit of Might came on all of them! (v. 31.)

Instead of hiding in their homes and asking God to slay their enemies, they got down on their faces and asked the Lord to grant them more boldness that they might

> ...**speak thy word,**
>
> **By stretching forth thine hand to heal; and that signs and wonders** [might] **be done by the name of thy holy child Jesus.**
>
> **Acts 4:29,30**

The Lord was so pleased with their response and request that the place where they were assembled was shaken, and they were all filled with the boldness of the Holy Spirit! (v. 31.)

They became united with one heart and one purpose, and none of them lacked anything. (vv. 32,33.)

And much to the horror of the religious, controlling leaders of that day, God gave great power to those who

43

believed. (v. 33.) That meant that more healings, more deliverances, and more salvation experiences took place in the city of Jerusalem after Peter and John had been threatened than before!

Let this be our testimony today. Ask God to fill you with the Spirit of Might so that you may blast through abusive, controlling spirits; then fulfill the plan and purpose of God in the earth!

6
Positive, Justifiable Control

Just as we have discussed the negative aspects of control, we need to study the positive nature of it as well. There is a good and justifiable control that God has ordained for our well-being. If it is of God, and we submit to it, positive control will groom us and shape us into maturity.

Justifiable control is characterized by moderation; good, sensible regulations; and restraints that bring excitement without the abuse of personal rights.

For example, the United States government has many controls that help protect the well-being and enhance the happiness of the American people. Some of these include: 1) drug laws, 2) immigration controls, and 3) federal regulations covering such vital matters as protection of public health, food inspection, conservation of natural resources, provision for education, and so forth.

If we do not allow ourselves to be controlled by proper moderation, regulations, and restraints, we will have problems with excesses. Positive, justifiable control serves as a godly balance in our lives.

We have a responsibility to God to follow mature, seasoned leadership. We are to be submitted to such leaders, to heed their wise counsel according to the Word of God. The greatest Teacher of all, the Holy Spirit, can reveal to us the attributes to look for in those who exercise godly, positive control.

The Holy Spirit

The Holy Spirit is still present on the earth today. His example in our lives should be the *standard* by which we pattern our relationship with others.

The Holy Spirit is the Controller of the life of the believer.

The Holy Spirit is not a dictator. He does not push us, pressure us, or smother our creativity. He is the Perfect Balance. We are created by God. The Holy Spirit gives us the freedom to express God through our own individual personalities.

The Holy Spirit will *convict* us of sin in our lives so we can be cleansed and go on with the plan of God unhindered. He will not *condemn* us, harass us, beat us down, or torment us, no matter how grievous our mistakes might be. God does not come to crush us, but to make us whole. His purpose is not to place us in bondage, but to set us free.

The Lord does not make our choices for us, nor does He harshly demand obedience from us. He does correct us, but it is always our choice to obey. In the book of John, Chapter 16, verse 13, we are told by Jesus:

> **Howbeit when he, the Spirit of truth, is come, he will *guide* you into all truth....**

The Holy Spirit is here to guide us into the truth of the Gospel. That is true and responsible leadership. He serves as a Conductor of the revelation of God in our lives. Notice that He will "guide" us, but it is our responsibility to follow His guidance.

Another characteristic of true godly leadership is found in the next part of that same verse:

> **...for he *shall not speak of himself*; but whatsoever he shall hear, that shall he speak: and he will shew you things to come.**

46

The Holy Spirit never points to Himself. He never exalts Himself or attempts to promote Himself. He is never in competition to be seen or heard. He speaks to us only what He hears from the Father, and if we will listen to Him and trust Him, He will tell us of things to come.

The first part of Romans 8:26 tells us more about the Holy Spirit and about good, positive control in our lives:

Likewise the Spirit also *helpeth* **our infirmities** [weaknesses]....

The Holy Spirit "helps" us. He will not do the job for us, neither will He expend all the effort needed to accomplish the task at hand. He will *help* us to fulfill the plan and purpose of God on the earth. A minister friend of mine once put it this way: "The Holy Spirit will *help* you do a job, just as I would *help* you move a chair. You pick up one side of the chair, and I lift the other. That is how the Holy Spirit helps the believer."

Positive control exercised through a person helps and guides, but it does not do so for self-gain. Positive control gives an individual the freedom, within the boundaries of the Word of God, to be himself and to express his own individual personality and creativity.

Positive control will never pressure, condemn, or smother. It will love and provide the encouragement needed to live life to the fullest for God. Positive control serves as a safety valve, a "check and balance," for our daily walk.

Positive Control Through Leadership

It is imperative that we understand one important principle: *God has always had a leader, and spiritual leaders must exercise legitimate, godly authority.*

Let's begin our study of this vital principle in the book of Ephesians, Chapter 4, verses 11 through 14. I like the way *The Amplified Bible* translates this passage:

And His gifts were [varied; He Himself appointed and gave men to us,] some to be apostles (special messengers), some prophets (inspired preachers and expounders), some evangelists (preachers of the Gospel, traveling missionaries), some pastors (shepherds of His flock) and teachers.

His intention was the *perfecting* and the *full equipping* of the saints (His consecrated people), [that they should do] the work of ministering toward building up Christ's body (the church),

[That it might develop] until we all attain oneness in the faith and in the comprehension of the full and accurate knowledge of the Son of God, that [we might arrive] at really mature manhood — the completeness of personality which is nothing less than the standard height of Christ's own perfection — the measure of the stature of the fullness of the Christ, and the completeness found in Him.

So then, we may no longer be children, tossed [like ships] to and fro between chance gusts of teaching, and wavering with every changing wind of doctrine, [the prey of] the cunning and cleverness of unscrupulous men, (gamblers engaged) in every shifting form of trickery in inventing errors to mislead.

Notice that it was the intention of the Lord to give certain leadership gifts to men and women to help the Body of Christ come into maturity and to know Him in an intimate way. These leadership gifts are often referred to as "the fivefold ministry."

These leaders are given gifts to help "equip" and "perfect" the believers. In Strong's concordance, the Greek word translated *perfecting* in this verse is derived from a root word meaning to "fit,...mend,...prepare, restore."[1]

---

[1]James Strong, *The Exhaustive Concordance of the Bible* (Nashville: Abingdon, 1890), "Greek Dictionary of the New Testament," p. 40, #2677.

Fit, mend, prepare, restore: These small words spell hard work and discipline. It is the job of the fivefold ministry to see to it that you and I are thoroughly endowed with faith, love, and hope, and fully equipped with the comprehension of the Son of God, the works and sensitivity of the Holy Spirit, and the knowledge of every other aspect of the Word of God. They are accountable to God for their leadership over us. We, in turn, are accountable for the degree of our submissiveness to that leadership.

Please understand that you and I are accountable to the *leadership* — the *office* and the *gifts* of the person — not the person himself. We are to follow the person as he or she follows the Word of God. When people in leadership positions are accurately demonstrating the Scriptures, we are accountable for how we submit to the gift inside them.

The Amplified Bible version of Hebrews 13:17 reads:

> **Obey your spiritual leaders and submit to them** — continually *recognizing their authority over you;* for they are constantly keeping watch over your souls and guarding your spiritual welfare, as men who will have to render an account [of their trust]. [Do your part to] let them do this with gladness, and not with sighing and groaning, for that would not be profitable to you [either].

In order for a leader to "fit," "mend," "prepare," and "restore" us, there must be some degree of positive, justifiable control over our lives. Refusal to submit to such protection and wisdom would mean outright rebellion on the part of the believer.

Because the Body of Christ has been vague on this issue, whenever strong leadership has surfaced the people have scattered shouting, "Control! Control!"

Let us as believers grow up and become mature. In this decade, we need *strong leadership.* The world does not hint at or suggest sin any longer. The world is blatant in its extremity. We, as the people of God, need to stand behind the strong leadership that God is raising up in our midst. We must follow these people as our examples in fulfilling the plan and purpose of heaven.

There are two attitudes the Church must "shake": 1) compromise on the part of its leaders, and 2) despising of and rebellion against strong leadership on the part of the people.

If leadership is not strong today, the Body of Christ will not grow to full maturity.

Leadership is positive action. It is not just talking; it is actually *doing* something. It is moving forward with the Lord and taking the people along as it goes.

As I was studying this subject, I was told that when the modern Israeli army goes into battle, its officers are sent in first; the troops then follow. This is said to be one of the reasons why the Israelis are so militarily successful: Their officers are out front, showing the troops which way to go and what to do. Other nations send their troops in first, while their leaders sit well behind the lines, viewing the battle through binoculars.

That is what some church leaders are doing today: They are trying to lead by remaining in the background. Part of this situation is the fault of the people because they do not understand good, godly, justifiable control. Whenever those in positions of leadership attempt to "fit, "mend," "prepare," or "restore" lives, the people develop a rebellious attitude and label the leadership as "controlling."

Remember that leaders are people too. They are human beings with real emotions and feelings just like everyone else. When they are continuously labeled and betrayed, they have a tendency to withdraw for protection against further hurts, wounds, and slander. If you are blessed with a strong leader, then follow that leader as he or she follows Christ.

Godly leadership will rise to the occasion and take the lead. When God speaks to leaders and tells their local body or nation to step out in an area of faith, they are bold to take action. Those believers who are sensitive to the Spirit of God, as well, will follow and support the cause with all their hearts.

Positive, justifiable control will confront the issues that are contrary to the purpose of God!

Many times when the Spirit of the Lord causes people to "step out," there will also be an extra grooming of their character, integrity, and faith. It is the job of the leader to instruct and discipline according to the Word of God. If you and I are to go on to full spiritual maturity, we must receive, submit, and grow. We must be willing to face the reality of where we stand spiritually, and then move on into maturity.

Leaders must not be afraid to confront any disorderly conduct that might take place in their services.

I am a strong believer in prayer and intercession, but many times some of the intercessors "get off" and begin to think they are the most spiritual people in the church. Some have even tried to use their positions to control the pastor or other leaders.

Every believer is called to the ministry of intercession. The reason some seem to be more anointed than others in the area of prayer is because they use it more! There is no scriptural reference to an "office of intercessor." An intercessor is a *servant of God* who is sensitive to His leadings to pray His will into the earth. An intercessor paves the way for the Holy Spirit to disarrange and thwart the schemes of the enemy. Prayers of intercession make the *plan* of God a *reality* for the hour.

Intercessors must be instructed in the spirit realm and in the Word of God in order to pray accurately in the will of God. Believers must be instructed in the ways and the character of God if they are to hear Him clearly. That is not abusive control! That is the positive control of the fivefold ministry.

Pastors must not be afraid to confront intercessors who are in error. They must not be hesitant to instruct them to pray decently and in order or else quit interceding in public worship until they can behave normally as they should.

I like leaders who are not afraid to confront and correct misdoing! That kind of godly boldness shows me that they value the Presence of the Holy Spirit in their midst. Such a positive confrontation reveals that the leader is committed to the maturity of the Body of Christ so that the world will be motivated to hunger for what we believers have.

In strong leadership there is security for the people of God. There is hope for the world through God's *strong* leaders and believers!

Religious, rebellious spirits do not like strong leadership! Such spirits want to dominate and control a church and its people.

If you have been confronted by a spiritual leader who has suggested that a change needs to take place in your personal life — rejoice and thank God for that individual!

Yes, the searing light of the Holy Spirit hurts our flesh at times, but it is for our own good. Our spiritual growth and maturity depend on it. As the Body of Christ, we are in training — so we must expect to be groomed and changed! Countless others are waiting to benefit from the training experience through which you and I will be successfully brought to full maturity.

Strong, positive control from a leader is an indication of his or her commitment to God. Do not rob yourself of the protection that God has ordained through those He has set in leadership positions in His Church.

We are an army, and in order to war effectively and triumphantly, we must be united in purpose and fervency. We must not break ranks in order to pamper our own soulish desires.

Do not shrink back from godly leaders who have given their lives for your benefit and maturity. Be thankful for godly direction in your life. What you learn from it will be your dearest treasure on the battlefield.

7

Positive Biblical Control

Let's look at a biblical story concerning strong leadership and a rebellious spirit that tried to prevail against it.

The Leadership of Moses

In the book of Numbers, Chapter 16, we find a very interesting situation. In the camp of the Israelites, there arose a man named Korah, a descendant of Levi, who went among the tribes complaining about the leadership of Moses. He thought Moses had taken too much power and authority upon himself as leader of God's people. In other words, Korah thought Moses was a "controller."

When Korah had secured enough backing from other disgruntled children of Israel, he and his followers approached Moses, God's chosen leader. In studying verse 2 of this passage, I find very interesting the type of people Korah recruited to join his cause:

> **And they rose up before Moses, with certain of the children of Israel, two hundred and fifty princes of the assembly, famous in the congregation, men of renown.**

Korah did not have God behind him, so he had to recruit the most famous men among the tribes of Israel in an attempt to give himself validity.

When these dissenters — including many of the other Levites who served in the temple worship — had assembled together, they approached Moses and Aaron. There Korah presented his accusation against these men of God:

> ...**Ye take too much upon you, seeing all the congregation are holy, every one of them, and the Lord is among them: wherefore then lift ye up yourselves above the congregation of the Lord?**
>
> **And when Moses heard it, he fell upon his face.**
>
> **Numbers 16:3,4**

Do these words sound familiar? "You are taking too much upon yourself, because everyone in this church is as holy as you are. Why are you lifting yourself up before the people? We can hear from God just as well as you can!"

These Israelites did not recognize the divine, positive control that had been given to Moses and Aaron by God Himself. Instead they were driven by jealousy, motivated by their desire for power, blinded to the truth by religion and rebellion.

Divine leadership involves a heavy price that must be paid in order to walk in the fullness of it. If it were not for the grace of God, the weight of it at times would be almost unbearable. The main price that must be paid by a leader concerns the daily life he or she must lead before the people. To walk in the fullness of divine authority — to exercise justifiable control — the leader is required to live in a certain way.

Divine leaders must pursue the way of righteousness and holiness. They must have a strong desire for God and hate evil with all of their hearts.

The devil wants to control the human will. If he can control a person's will, he can control the person. Compromise will weaken an individual's ability to take a strong stand against Satan.

When you and I are strong and refuse to bow to evil and wrong, there will be those who will try to find something wrong with us in order to destroy our character, undermine our stand, and overcome our strength. But divine leaders must pay the price of faithfulness, no matter what comes against them. It is a price that causes heaven to take notice. God will move the foundations of the earth for the faithful.

Divine leaders must walk in accuracy and discernment in the Spirit. They will not change their stand just because they are under attack from the enemy; they will continue to obey God in the midst of conflict and adversity.

After Moses had heard the accusation levied against him and Aaron by Korah and his followers, he fell on his face before the Lord. Then he rose up to speak to Korah and the sons of Levi who were with him:

> Seemeth it but a small thing unto you, that the God of Israel hath separated you from the congregation of Israel, to bring you near to himself to do the service of the tabernacle of the Lord, and to stand before the congregation to minister unto them?
>
> And he hath brought thee near to him, and with all thy brethren the sons of Levi with thee: and seek ye the priesthood also?
>
> Numbers 16:9,10

What Moses was asking them is simply this: "Is it nothing to you that the Lord has chosen you to stand in His house and minister to Him before the people? Do you see your place in the Body as such a minor thing? And having (obviously) failed at that, do you actually think you have *paid the price* to stand in the office of the priesthood?"

When Korah and the Levites refused to listen to the reasoning of Moses, the man of God proclaimed, "Tomorrow the Lord will show who is His chosen leader." (v. 5.)

After he had gone before the Lord, Moses was instructed by God to have the people choose the side they were on: Korah's or Moses'. After the children of Israel had run to whichever side they had chosen, Moses stood before them and declared:

> ...Hereby ye shall know that the Lord hath sent me to do all these works; for I have not done them of mine own mind.

> Numbers 16:28

He continued to speak, warning the people that if the Lord was on his side, the earth would open up and swallow the rebellious Korah and his group because they had provoked the Lord their God. The Bible records that as soon as Moses had finished speaking, the earth did open up and swallow Korah, his people, and all his goods; so they vanished from the congregation. God then sent a fire to consume the 250 murmurers who had gathered with Korah. (vv. 30-35.)

God will never forsake the godly leaders He has ordained, no matter who or what should rise up against them. Moses continually showed his heart for the people in the face of God; then he confronted the people with bold leadership in order to turn them back to the Lord.

The Leadership of Paul

The ministry of the Apostle Paul is another example of positive, justifiable control in the area of leadership.

In First Corinthians, Chapter 4, beginning with verse 15, Paul makes a very bold statement:

> For though ye have ten thousand instructors in Christ, yet have ye not many fathers: for in Christ Jesus I have begotten you through the gospel.

> Wherefore I beseech you, be ye followers of me.

> 1 Corinthians 4:15,16

Look at the security Paul enjoyed in his position as a leader! He told the church in Corinth which he had established, "Even though you have heard many teachers and preachers, I am the one who led you to spiritual birth. Therefore, follow my example and lifestyle.''

How many of us would say that Paul practiced abusive control? *None of us!* Yet I dare say that if a leader today should make such a bold statement as this one by Paul, many would have him labeled before the sun came up!

Again, look at what Paul said in his letter to the church in Philippi:

> **Brethren, be followers together of me, and mark them which walk so as ye have us for an ensample.**
>
> **Philippians 3:17**

Not only did Paul tell the Philippian believers to follow his lifestyle, he also said that they should watch those who followed him, for they were good examples of Christianity. That is secure leadership!

As a leader chosen and anointed by God, Paul took his responsibility seriously. He watched carefully over the flock of believers under his authority, and many times he wrote to them, ''Although I am not there with you in the flesh, know that I am with you in spirit.'' Second Corinthians 11:2 reveals the intensity with which Paul related to his flock:

> **For I am jealous over you with godly jealousy: for I have espoused you to one husband, that I may present you as a chaste virgin to Christ.**

As a leader, Paul was ''jealous'' over those he had brought to Jesus. He was constantly on guard against anyone or anything that might come to steal the people of God away from their First Love — Jesus Christ. He fought against the sin that might blemish the Church. He did not hesitate to confront because of the love he had for Jesus. He wanted everyone who believed to come into the full maturity that the resurrection had provided for them. He took the risk of being hated, persecuted, and killed so that lives could be saved. That's not abusive control — *that is positive, justifiable, godly leadership!*

59

Paul never desired or sought to be exalted by men. He was a true servant of God. In the book of Galatians, Chapter 1, I believe he revealed his true heart as he gave the account of his salvation and training experience. He had done great works for the Lord, but as he finished relating the story, he said this of the people who had heard him speak:

And they glorified God *in* me.

Galatians 1:24

The whole key to positive, biblical control is the fact that — no matter how many decisions we make, how many conversions we produce, how many people are healed or delivered by our message, how many foes we conquer — our primary concern is that Jesus Christ be seen first and foremost in every situation we face.

8
Are You a Controller?

We have learned the attributes of both negative, abusive control and positive, justifiable control. Since we now have this understanding, it is important to rid ourselves of any tendencies we may have in the negative areas. Learning these things about control will cause some of us to think immediately of people we know who are controllers.

But what if you suspect that *you* may have a controlling personality? How can you recognize whether you have a tendency to be an abusive controller?

1. You have a tendency to be an abusive controller if you feel that the only way you can be important or accepted is by giving orders and making demands.

Do not allow ambition and a desire for power to "drive" you. Ambition and power-seeking will not produce godly authority. In the book of Matthew, Chapter 8, Jesus marveled at the humility of a Roman centurion. Beginning in verse 8, we read this exchange between Jesus and this military leader:

> **The centurion answered and said, Lord, I am not worthy that thou shouldest come under my roof: but speak the word only, and my servant shall be healed.**
>
> **For I am a man under authority, having soldiers under me: and I say to this man, Go, and he goeth; and to another, Come, and he cometh; and to my servant, Do this, and he doeth it.**
>
> **Matthew 8:8,9**

Jesus replied that He had not found such faith in all of Israel. (v. 10.) This man had learned the principle of godly leadership and authority. In his humility to those in authority over him, he had become an authority himself. He was a trusted leader, one whose commands could be followed and fulfilled.

When we submit ourselves to God, He will lift us up in due season. When that season comes, our sense of worth will come from a trust in Him, not from our ability to give orders or commands.

2. You have a tendency to be an abusive controller if you feel possessive about a person or persons, if you feel that others have to "check in" with you because you know more than they do or what is best for them, if you never accept their judgment of what they think they should do, or if you always belittle them because you are convinced they don't know anything.

Possessive people always try to make others feel that they don't know anything, that they are totally ignorant and immature. Possessive controllers make others feel that the only way they are going to survive is by consulting with them and doing what they say.

When anyone voices an opinion to them, they cut that individual down by saying, "Oh, that isn't true. You're wrong; I'm right."

One sure sign that you are an abusive controller is if you never allow any differing opinions or ideas to be discussed, accepted, or even expressed. The other person's voice goes in one ear and out the other, while you continue to "do your own thing."

3. You have a tendency to be an abusive controller if you begin to feel intense jealousy over another person, especially if that jealousy dominates your opinions and actions.

For example, if the person you have been controlling starts talking to someone else, you will automatically feel jealous, possessive and threatened, and you will probably try to cut off that relationship. You will intrude into the conversation in order to monitor it!

4. *You have a tendency to be an abusive controller if you feel threatened by another person's new relationships.*

You are a controller if you feel that your friendship and relationship with another person are threatened if he or she speaks to someone else, prays with another individual, goes out to dinner with somebody besides you, or engages in any other activity with anyone but you — even for as little as five minutes.

Remember, *commitment isn't control!*

This discussion is limited to people in friendship relationships, not to people in marriages. A married person's best friend should be his or her mate. A married couple has made a commitment to each other in the sight of God and man. A certain amount of exclusiveness is an implied part of marriage. We will discuss this issue in a later chapter.

5. *You have a tendency to be an abusive controller if you feel that you must protect the other person from every experience.*

Let's discuss this topic in more detail. If you feel that you must shield a person from life's experiences, then you are guilty of *carrying his or her responsibilities.* Every individual must be accountable for his own behavior. Instead, a controller attempts to shield another from personal responsibility, often then turning around and getting angry with the other person for not being more responsible. The controller then feels used, cheated, and abused.

This kind of overprotection can happen in any relationship, especially between a parent and child. When an individual has reached maturity, protecting him or her from life's experiences is a *destructive* form of helping. The Bible says that godly wisdom and understanding come from God's Word and life's experiences. (Prov. 3:13 AMP.)

Experiences, both good and bad, groom our character and cause us to walk in the wisdom of God. The varied experiences of life, coupled with the Word of God, season us and bring us understanding.

If you are guilty of "shielding" another from an experience he or she has chosen, then no character is formed in that individual. It will be a never-ending cycle of protection. Everyone will end up feeling frustrated and abused.

An abusive controller is one who tries to "fix" people's feelings, do their thinking for them, or solve their problems for them.

I am not talking about a genuine act of love and respect. I am speaking of an unnatural drive to take responsibility for someone else. This behavior is actually an insult to the other person. The abusive controller is making a statement that the other individual is incompetent and incapable of making a choice or decision for himself.

In such cases, usually the other person has never asked the controller for help. That is why the controller gets angry when the other person goes on his way, seemingly ungrateful.

Most abusive controllers truly believe they are helping others when they shield them from experiences. They may even think it is cruel or heartless to let others face up to their own dilemmas.

Many controllers even twist and contort the Scriptures on love and giving as they relate to abusive control. But the Word of God should set us free — not hold us in bondage.

Jesus held people accountable for fulfilling their own responsibilities. Notice throughout the Gospels how Jesus Himself reacted to those who came to Him seeking healing, deliverance or some other miracle. He always responded to the needs of people by asking them a question — for He knew that the answer they gave would reveal the true nature of their hearts.

Each of us must go through our own experiences in life. But we are not helpless! Jesus Christ has given us a gift — the resurrection power of the Holy Spirit living inside of us. And that's not all. The power of His Spirit within will guide us into truth and victory!

You must also understand that a controlling person thinks and talks about the other individual all the time. If anything keeps the other person from spending time with the controller, the controller will attack that thing and attempt to get rid of it as quickly as possible. He will go to any length or any expense to make sure the person he is controlling spends the majority of his or her time with him.

This is *domination*!

The controlling person will dominate the other individual's vacations, dates, marriage, job, home-buying, church-going, or even personal finances. An abusive controller will dominate every area of another's life if allowed to do so.

If the other person is not careful, he or she can become so entwined with a controller that, in extreme cases, it will take years to get free of that relationship.

6. You have a tendency to be an abusive controller if you react in an unnatural way to statements made about the person you are controlling.

For example, if someone makes a positive statement about the person you control, you will automatically criticize the controlled person to make sure that no friendship develops between them.

On the other hand, if someone makes a negative statement about you, the controller, you will immediately defend yourself with a positive statement to make yourself look good.

7. You have a tendency to be an abusive controller if you attempt to overprotect — even to the point of hindering God's Spirit.

For example, sometimes elders or deacons can be so protective of the church that they won't allow the pastor to flow under the anointing of the Lord; they won't help him do what God has told him to do.

Individually, an abusive controller can be so protective of another person that he will not allow that individual to venture out and experience God for himself or herself. The abusive controller is afraid that the person being controlled will make a mistake; therefore, fear is the core motivation for every decision.

Because fear is the motive in overprotection, positive growth, whether individual or corporate, is hindered.

8. You have a tendency to be an abusive controller if you make plans for the other person without his or her permission.

An abusive controller actually makes plans for the other person without even asking permission to do so! If the individual who is being controlled doesn't want to follow the plan, he is usually made to feel so guilty that he ends up going along with it anyway. He knows that if he doesn't agree, all hell will break loose!

Has a relative ever volunteered your services on a certain project without your permission? You knew that if you didn't agree, there would be a war in the family for weeks. That's control. Many families are so controlled that they never enjoy a normal life.

God did not design human beings to live a miserable life under someone else's control, following someone else's plans and designs for their lives. *Each person was meant to live his or her own life with God. If anyone thinks he has a right to control another person's life in order to assure his or her success, that is a lie!*

9. You have a tendency to be an abusive controller if you think the person you control owes you something, and you demand that it be paid back.

Here is an example of this kind of control. A mom and dad have a boy, Rick, who has been a very good son. He hasn't been rebellious in any way. He feels a call to the ministry, but because he enters Bible school or seminary instead of engineering school, his parents have a fit! They want him to have "security" in life.

They nag, cry, interfere, and generally do everything they can to get Rick to change his mind, leave school, return to his hometown, and enroll at the local state university. (They also want him to live at home, of course, so they can continue to "supervise" him.") They stress their belief that he "owes" them this consideration because they are his parents and have devoted their lives to rearing him.

This a perfect example of *control versus call.*

Such people fail to see that the call of God on an individual's life is the highest calling in life! There is a way to biblically "honor" one's parents and still go on with God. He is the One Who must be answered to. Rick must follow Elisha's advice, respectfully kiss his parents good-bye, and follow God. (1 Kings 19:20.) The Lord will take care of the rest.

If you and I do our best to be obedient to the call of God upon our lives, everything else will eventually fall into place. Learn to trust God.

10. You have a tendency to be an abusive controller if you try to manipulate people through use of flattery.

Actually, if you are a controller you can go to the extreme in either direction. You can cut others down so low with your words that they feel that if they don't do what you say, you might write "infidel" across their foreheads. Or you can use honeyed words to flatter people into complying with your wishes and desires.

This is the way some ministries grow. The preacher not only controls his people through flattery, he also gets money out of them by the same means! He "pumps them up" by telling them how much he and God love them.

Yet such people won't help the girl who has had an abortion. They won't cast the homosexual demon out of anyone. They won't minister to those plagued with AIDS. They don't want mixed nationalities or races in their congregations. They refuse to receive certain types of people in their churches because it doesn't look "nice."

Ministers have to be careful not to flatter one another to get the speakers and support they desire and need. We must never forget that it is God Who exalts, and it is God Who brings down.

In *The Amplified Bible* version, Daniel 11:32 states of the Antichrist:

And such as violate the covenant he shall pervert and seduce with flatteries....

We have a covenant with God regarding the plan and destiny for our lives. Those who do not recognize God as their sole Source and Security will fall victim to flattery.

But the good news is that this verse goes on!

...but the people who know their God shall prove themselves strong and shall stand firm, and do exploits....

Whether as a believer or a leader, your personal security should depend on God, and God alone. Being secure in the Lord will enhance your other relationships. A ministry will never grow unless God is the Security, Foundation, and Source of it.

We must lie down with our faces bowed before God and cry out to Him. We must not be afraid to go before the Lord and give Him our troubles and cares. In return, He will fill us with His strength. Giving "our all" to God means just that: turning over to Him every part of us, and then *leaving it there* with Him, trusting Him to handle it for us.

Faithful is he that calleth you, who also will do it.

1 Thessalonians 5:24

That is why we give ourselves to God. "Self" cannot be our Source or our Comfort. That is why we say, "It is not some of self and some of God; *it is none of self and all of God.*"

9
Control by Parents

In the next three chapters, we will discuss the main "hot spots" of control. We will examine the negative and the positive aspects of control in these vital areas.

As we have seen, controlling spirits most often attempt to work through the people nearest us — even family members — rather than through strangers.

We must be careful that the normal control in a family situation — such as the natural control that the Bible indicates a parent is to exercise over a child — does not become unnatural or abusive.

Adults in a family can consciously or unconsciously limit a young person's ability to succeed in life. This happens because of negative, fearful, or even unscriptural family attitudes or "customs."

In First Timothy 1:4, Paul stated that "endless genealogies" should be avoided. If something is to be avoided, it is because it is harmful.

According to Strong's concordance, the Greek word translated *genealogies* in this verse is partially derived from a root word used to refer to "something *said, . . . reasoning, . . .* or *motive.*"[1]

"Endless genealogies" can be boundaries of limitations inherited from family members or handed down through family philosophy and tradition. Many times a response or

---

[1] James Strong, *The Exhaustive Concordance of the Bible* (Nashville: Abingdon, 1890), "Greek Dictionary of the New Testament," p. 20, #1076.

reaction comes from a motive shadowed by spirits of poverty, fear, or bitterness. These motivating spirits in a family will cause an abusive control to dominate it, sometimes for generations. In order to succeed in the fullness that God has for each of us, we must break these controlling spirits and nullify their effects upon us.

Some examples of the responses motivated by such controlling spirits are:

1. "No one in this family may ever buy a new car, only a used one."

2. "No one in this family will ever leave our church or denomination, because our grandfather helped establish it."

3. "No one in this family may marry without the approval of the other family members; no one is allowed to follow his or her own heart in these matters."

Every family has its "weak spots," no matter how spiritual it may seen in other areas. In our own families, we must discover these spots and turn them back to the strength of God, in Jesus' name.

"Endless genealogies" often become controlling factors in the way people live and train their children. However, Christian couples should not rear their children this way. Believers need to break away from these ungodly hindrances and limitations, training their children in the victory and likeness of Christ!

Training your children is your responsibility and your commitment to them. It is living in front of them, teaching them, and directing their lives by word and example. Training is not a smothering, overprotective, fearful control.

A Time for Parents To Let Go

The writer of the book of Ecclesiastes says that there is a time for everything under the sun. (Eccl. 3:1.) *That means that when children grow up and choose a life partner, it is time for parents to let go of them and to respect their marriage!*

When parents refuse to do this, it causes major problems. When parents visit the newlyweds and tell them what they should or should not do, it causes problems. When grandchildren are born and the grandparents start telling the parents how to rear their children, it causes even more problems.

When a couple asks their parents or in-laws for advice, it should be given; but unless their advice is sought, parents should keep quiet and pray! Unfortunately, some parents can't wait to be consulted; they just barge in and tell their children how to live.

Parental interference causes friction in marriages, and that is how some marital problems begin.

The tragedy is, some marriages never survive this interference, because one of the partners is unable to break a parent's control over his or her life.

It is sad to say that some divorces are actually caused by interfering parents!

I am not saying that every in-law is a potential problem-maker, but in-laws who attempt to control their children do cause problems. The most prevalent in-law problem is found in controlling parents who won't release their daughter or son. Such people have no trust in their own training of their children.

It is true that such parents are truly concerned about the proper training and upbringing of their offspring; *the problem is that their sense of security and self-worth is vested in their son or daughter, rather than in their relationship with the Living God.*

73

When the child is out on his own, it causes the parents to realize that their source of security, which is the child, is now lost — and they don't know what to do. They are no longer around him all the time to monitor and control his actions. They are living in such insecurity that they go into a frenzy!

Parents, if your children are married, release them to God. Look at the situation realistically. When you and your mate were first married, you had to find out how to live and make it together as one family. You both made right choices and wrong choices. You had rocky roads and smooth roads. You spent money wisely and sometimes foolishly. When the romance seemed to leave the marriage, you were stuck together by commitment until the romance sparked again. You had to discover together how to build a strong unit and call it a "family."

Give your children the freedom to discover life with *their mates on their own.* If they come to you and your mate for advice, give it. But after it is given, leave your children alone to make their own decisions with their mates. Let them be responsible to live their own lives as adults. If you have trained your children by the Word of God, then *you* are not their Foundation — God is — and you should rest in that fact.

Look at this time in your life as a fresh, new start of enjoyment for you and your mate. It is never too late to develop security in God and to begin a new adventure in life. It will take work, because so much of your married life has revolved around and centered upon your children; but you can do it.

Allow the Holy Spirit to show you how to pray for your children's marriages, and be a support to them. The days ahead can be the best ones of your life, if you will make the right decision today to "love, let go, and live."

10
Control by Spouses

An overbearing husband destroys the life of his wife and children. An overbearing wife destroys the life of her husband and children.

That's why many children leave home as soon as they reach the age of 16 — or even younger! If parents do not leave room for their children to experience joy outside of their parental authority — if youngsters cannot live without their parents breathing down their necks all the time — there will be problems in the family.

No, I don't mean that children should be allowed to do whatever they want to do! This message must be understood in the Spirit in order to achieve a proper balance in life. People who don't have balance in their lives slide into errors of carnality or "super-spirituality."

"Submit, Submit, Submit!"

Some husbands who have no spiritual balance in their lives turn their wives into weary, battered "nobodies." It is not exciting to live with a "doormat." Most of these women were not that way when their husbands first met them. But eventually, because their mates were always yelling at them, "Submit, submit, submit," they did. The constant demands and the abusive control they endured for so long finally caused them to submit to the point that now they barely exist.

This is definitely *not* the plan of God for marriage. There are all sorts of insecurities that would cause a husband to dominate his wife in this way.

Some of these hurt and wounded wives decided that they needed to protect themselves, so they became involved in the feminist movement. Some joined because of ignorant, insensitive husbands who were always yelling at them, "Submit, submit, submit!"

On the other hand, some women are just as selfish and self-centered as these men. I once met a pastor's wife who did nothing but consume soft drinks and watch soap operas. She would not cook breakfast for her children, help them get off to school, or make any effort to clean the house. She didn't believe that any of these tasks were her job.

If a husband and wife will just flow together in the Spirit, there will be no question of "whose job is this?" and "whose job is that?" When there is love in a marriage, there is mutual consideration. The partners aren't selfish; they help each other.

Abusive control and domination cause the loss of human dignity. In such a marriage, the controlled partner doesn't become a "help mate"; he or she becomes a "slave mate." And that must stop.

There is a true, biblical attitude of submission on the part of a wife toward her husband. That kind of submission is of God, but it is nothing like that which is demanded by a selfish, overbearing companion.

I have met many women who cannot do anything unless their husbands approve of it. They live in constant fear of making their mates angry. Such women are afraid to breathe without permission. They exist in a tight circle that is limited by the things their husbands allow them to do. All these women can say is, "Whatever you want, dear."

That's not being submissive; that's being a robot!

This kind of dependent relationship is smothering and unnatural. It is based on insecurity, and is in danger of destruction. Too much dependency will drive a person away. No one can protect his or her position and security by being overly dependent. We human beings were made to express life and to fulfil the purpose of our Creator in the earth. Anything that hinders that kind of "life flow" will eventually self-destruct.

Remember: God is our Source and Comfort in every area of life. Every prospering relationship stems from that revelation inside of us.

Portrait of a Control Victim

Several years ago as I was ministering in a church to which I had been invited to speak, I met a woman who was, unfortunately, a perfect example of a control victim.

Before the service that evening, I was sitting at my book table in the back of the church, because I like to talk with people.

As I sat there, I watched this woman enter the building. She was pushing ahead of her, like a flock of geese, three rowdy children under five years of age. They were just toddlers, with all the energy and abandon of their age. They were doing everything all at the same time: screaming, hollering, laughing and crying — the "whole works." It takes two parents even to attempt to corral this many young dynamos, and this woman was trying to do it all alone.

Then I saw the door shut behind a man who had a mean look on his face. What I saw shocked my spirit. I thought to myself, "Something is wrong with this man; maybe he's oppressed."

The woman really had her hands full, so I walked down the aisle and helped her take off the children's coats. She didn't know that I was the visiting preacher.

"I wonder where my husband is," she said with a strained look on her face. "Oh, there he is!"

Guess who the husband was. The man who had walked through the door and caused my spirit to sound off like an alarm: *"There's something wrong...something wrong...something wrong...!"*

The man had already found a seat. He didn't even stand up to help his family enter the row. He just pulled back his knees so they could squeeze through on their way to their seats. In the process, one youngster "escaped" and began running down the aisles. I picked him up and plopped him in his father's lap, saying, "Here's your child."

As I did so, I noticed that neither the wife nor the children were dressed very well, but that the man was wearing a nice suit.

Controllers Like To Be Served

Controllers try to act like God, because *controlling spirits make people serve their own selfish needs and desires.* Controllers are never considerate of others. This is the hardest thing to get a controller to understand, because in his eyes he is so wonderful and so right. He thinks he loves everybody, because everybody serves *him*. This idea is totally false, of course.

That night I preached a sermon on control, and to be perfectly honest I directed it right at this man.

After the time of worship, the woman came up to the front of the church and stood in the prayer line. As I laid hands on her and began to pray for her, I felt a "reaction" in her husband, even though he was still back in the congregation, and withdrew my hands from her.

"We've got a big one here tonight!" I thought. "This is a major controlling spirit."

So I laid my hands on the woman's head again, and this time I was determined not to budge because I knew she wanted to be free.

"I need your help," she whispered to me. "You're the first preacher who has let me know what I'm in. I thought my husband and I were living the way we were supposed to, but then I saw that other people's marriages were not like ours."

This woman wasn't talking about material things. She was referring to the normal interaction between husband and wife: loving each other, holding hands, taking care of the children together — enjoying life with one another. That's what people get married for!

As I was praying for her, she got in the Spirit and began to be set free. Her face started to glow. But then something struck her soul with a shock! It was her husband's controlling spirit reacting.

"Don't get upset," I told her. "Just flow with the Spirit. God says that He wants you to be free."

It was almost half an hour before she was able to keep her freedom in the Spirit. By the anointing of God through prayer, she was able to see her value as a person. With the Word of God and scriptural counseling from their church, this couple's marriage was eventually made whole.

Leaders Should Deal With Controllers

The leaders in that church should have dealt with that problem years earlier. We are brothers and sisters in Christ, and when there is a situation among us as bad as this one which goes on and on, the church elders and deacons should help the pastor confront it and restore liberty and peace to those affected by it. That is part of their job.

If you are forced to deal with a situation like this one, don't advertise the fact — just do it! The controlling husband or wife may react violently at first (any evil spirit will "blow up" when confronted directly), but deal with the problem with love and firmness — in the power of the Holy Spirit.

11
Control by Money

Just as control works most often through the *people* closest to the victim, so it also works through the *thing* closest to the one being controlled. The saying is true: "If God has your heart, He has your money." We must be sure that *we* direct our money; we must not allow money to direct us or dictate to us.

There is another saying: "He who pays the piper calls the tune." There is a great deal of truth to this quote as well.

A number of people will be able to control you through money during your lifetime.

It started when you were a child. Your parents exerted a certain amount of control over your behavior through your allowance. You were probably expected to perform certain tasks around the house, in the yard, or on the farm, if you lived in the country, in exchange for your allowance.

Later in life, your bosses exerted a great deal of control over your behavior and job performance through your salary. These kinds of control through money are normal, as long as they are not excessive in any way.

Parents — especially well-to-do parents — also use money as a means to control their adult children. Spouses too use money as a lever of control — especially at the present time, when both partners in a marriage usually work.

Another controlling influence that may never have occurred to you is *debt*. Being in debt means that you are, to some extent, under the control of other people. Debt can restrict the joy and achievement level of people's lives — and the pressure of debt can wreck marriages!

We must be cautious in the area of debt, that it does not consume us. Debt is a "sneaky" hinderance. It can creep upon us and ruin our lives if we are not wise to it. Satan can use this means to bind the Church and hinder us from supporting and giving to the work of the Lord around the world. We must be on our guard against this evil, because we are to finance the Gospel in the earth.

In this hour of shaky economy, we must operate totally by God's laws of giving and receiving. (Luke 6:38; Mal. 3:10.) Be wise in your financial and business dealings so you and your family can enjoy life on God's beautiful earth without the restraints of overwhelming debt.

Control by Money in the Church

The above examples of financial control are common and often discussed. However, we will consider control through money in a far different way — as it affects the local church.

Unfortunately, in many churches there are frequently found prominent members who are really "into" control by their money. They somehow think that if they give large tithes and offerings, then they have a right to issue orders. If everyone doesn't do exactly as they desire, they react.

If the pastor so much as preaches two minutes beyond twelve noon, they may threaten to reduce or withhold their offerings. If the pastor is not strong, and his security is in money, he may quickly knuckle under to this type of financial pressure and agree to do anything demanded of him — without praying first or discussing the situation with the Lord — just to keep that large donation coming in! Such a pastor is depending upon flesh rather than on God.

Money is not head of the Church — *Jesus Christ is the Head of the Church!*

These prominent people need to learn that money is not given to the church to purchase power and prestige: money is given to God as an expression of *love!*

The giving of money to God should be an established way of life for the believer.

Giving is one means of showing God that we understand that He owns everything and that He has given good things to us and our household. We worship God with our money because of what it represents — total submission of our lives to Him. When we give our money, that act shows God, heaven, and the devil just Who our Source is. Giving is a means of fulfilling a part of the covenant between us and the Lord, demonstrating that it is He, and not we ourselves, Who has given us the power to get wealth. (Deut. 8:18.)

Now you may be thinking, "God didn't give me my money; I worked hard for it myself." God gave you the breath of life so you could get up and go to work. He gave you strength to move and a brain to think creatively. If it were not for Him, you couldn't even go to work!

There is a whole world of revelation in the giving of money to God. Begin to ask the Holy Spirit to teach you the lifestyle of giving to God. Find the giving and tithing scriptures in the Word of God, in both the Old and New Testaments. Study them and meditate on them until they become a revelation and a way of life to you.

God is not in a box, nor is He a taskmaster when it comes to giving.

One particular couple had gotten in such terrible debt, they were unable to tithe and continue living on a daily basis. They couldn't let even one bill go unpaid without destroying their future. So what did the Holy Spirit direct them to do? *Begin tithing toward the tithe!*

This couple wanted so desperately to restore themselves in the area of giving that they began to tithe a small percentage toward what their normal tithe would be. They sowed seeds toward their financial restoration! As a result, today they give to their church over and above the required amount.

Money and debt do not have to control you. There is always a way, through the Holy Spirit, to recover.

When I started preaching this message, people who are acting as money controllers began to react *immediately*! Do not let such people bother or hinder you. Do not allow money to control you. Be free in your giving, so you can be free in your mind. When you see how God blesses your finances, you will grow in faith.

Control Hinders the Flow of the Spirit

One principle in which God carefully trained me in the beginning of my ministry is not to depend on people's giving to pay my ministry expenses.

A frequent problem in the modern church is the fact that some preachers are dependent upon people's giving. They get so controlled by money that they lose the real flow of the Spirit!

This is one reason why some congregations are not going on with God. A few people with controlling spirits are running things in the church, and the pastor doesn't want to lose them, because they are so influential in the city. However, their control, if not changed, will stop the move of God in that church!

Pastors have a need to be liked. Every person and every minister has that desire, but especially pastors because they are "planted" among the people they serve. Unlike the traveling evangelist, they can't come through town, blast out a sermon, and leave the next day! If a pastor is not secure in God, he will preach messages which the Lord has not told him to deliver, simply because he doesn't want to offend the influential, well-to-do members of his congregation. God doesn't instruct ministers to preach "people-pleasing" sermons.

As ministers, we must preach the fresh Word of the Lord; and it isn't always what the people want to hear! Having a big church is one thing, but compromising to have one produces a large, stagnant church without the power and glory of God.

A minister must realize that God is his Source, not a prominent person with money. If you are a minister who is being controlled by someone with money in your church, this is what you should do: Hand the money back and say to those who are attempting to control you with it, "Here's your money. God is my Source. If your motive in giving is not to use your money to serve the Lord and His Church, then go someplace else where you can do what you want."

And that is what that person will do — he won't come to church for a while. He may not even speak to you, but if he does, he will say things like: "Who do you think you are, coming to our town? I was here long before you were ever voted in, Pastor!"

Here's something important to remember: *Pastors are not voted in; God sets them in the Church.*

Furthermore, the pastor — not the flock — is the undershepherd of that congregation. The elders and deacons are to give the pastor counsel, advice and physical and spiritual support, but the pastor is not obligated to follow that counsel and advice if the Spirit of God leads otherwise.

Using Money To Control the Preacher

I had an interesting experience with one of these controlling types once. He offered me money if I would get up and retract what I had just preached about removing proud members of the church board! I had said, "If a deacon or an elder cannot flow with the spirit of God, then he should be removed from the board."

After this man had offered me the bribe, I replied, "I won't retract what I said, because it was right. But you can give me the money anyway."

He didn't do it. I found out later than he was the problem in the church!

This man wanted me to retract that statement and the anointed words that convicted people of their sin. *He wanted to see if he could manipulate me.*

Sometimes people come up to me after a service, complaining to me and wanting me to withdraw something I have said. If I am wrong about something, I will apologize. If I have said something that is not right, I will retract the statement. However, I will not withdraw from the anointing, and I will not apologize for being right.

If you apologize for something you said while under the anointing, it weakens your anointing and power. It causes you to falter in your stand and strength. The truth is the truth. When you stand with the truth, you will be right with God and right with the people.

12

How To Be Free From Control

There is freedom for those who are bound by control. Whether you have been the controller or the person being controlled, you *can* be set free!

Regardless of the degree of control you are under, you need to be set free, because you can't live a happy, normal life if you are being controlled by someone else.

How do you break the power of control? You must break your habit of unnatural expectations toward another person. You must break the power of fear over you, in Jesus' name.

Steps Toward Freedom

If you are being controlled by someone else, here are some steps you can take to free yourself from that situation.

1. Recognize that you are being controlled.

Let's examine some of the ways you can know if you are being controlled by another person.

When you are around the other individual, you are not yourself. You feel intimidated, and you grow increasingly ill at ease around him or her. You wish your relationship were as happy and free as others you see.

You feel insecure and inadequate when you try to do new things on your own. Your hopes can be totally dashed and your mind thrown into confusion and instability if the other person makes just one negative statement, such as, ''I don't think you can do that.''

You feel obligated to spend time with the other person, even though he or she has no consideration for your schedule or lifestyle.

As soon as you return from a pleasant outing with friends or acquaintances, the other person, because he or she was not invited, feels threatened and attacks you. The individual may even try to "spiritualize" the attack by saying, "I've been in the Spirit and I know what went on while you were gone." He or she will offer you a list of things about yourself that aren't true, and if you aren't careful you will end up agreeing with them.

When you are pulled between two opinions, yours and the other person's, you feel obligated to agree. You lose your human dignity to the point that you become careless about your appearance and lose your strong desire to be successful in life. You look and feel listless and exhausted.

2. *Recognize how that person controls you.*

Is it through fear, guilt, obligation, anger, tears, frustration, confusion or any of the other things we have discussed? Whatever it may be, find it and break its power over you, in Jesus' name. Locate the scriptures that strengthen you against these negative influences. Say them aloud over and over until they become a part of you. When the controlling attack comes, you will then be able to counterattack it through the Word of God.

3. *Determine and apply the correction you need in your thought patterns and actions in order to stop the control from dominating your life.*

For example, if you are controlled through silence, learn not to respond to it. Don't feel guilty when the controller doesn't speak to you for days on end. Go on and enjoy life. Let the other person be miserable if that is what he or she chooses. Sooner or later the controller will realize that silence can no longer be an effective method to control you.

Often a husband will refuse to speak to his wife (or vice versa) because of something she said that he didn't agree with. He uses this childish weapon to punish her instead of discussing the problem like an adult and resolving the issue so they can live in peace and harmony. Personally, I don't understand how two people can live together in the same house with this kind of strife going on between them.

Disharmony hinders the movement of the Spirit of God.

Even if a tiny "irk" occurs among my ministerial staff, we deal with it and get rid of it immediately, because we know that *the Holy Spirit will not flow through a clogged pipe!*

When you are grieved and hurt, the Holy Spirit cannot speak or heal through you. In order to hear accurately in the Spirit realm, you must be free from the hurts and bondages that may come in life.

Another way a controller may try to dominate you is through words of inadequacy or failure, such as, "You can't do that; you don't know how. You'll just fail because you're not educated."

Remind the controller that many people thought that Albert Einstein was mentally retarded as a child, and that Abraham Lincoln suffered nothing but defeats and setbacks for years before he became a successful statesman. In fact, many of the most successful people in life never earned an academic degree. So don't let your past history of failures or your lack of formal education keep you from becoming all that God intends for you.

A controller may even use threats against you, such as, "If you don't do what I say, I'm going to leave you!"

Don't be intimidated by such negative remarks. Remember that the Greater One lives in you, and that you are important to God. Attack those evil spirits by reminding them of who you are in Christ Jesus.

Again, find scriptures to support you in your battle. Matthew 4:10 is a good one. The devil came to Jesus demanding that He fall down and worship him. Jesus answered, . . . **Get thee hence, Satan: for it is written, Thou shalt worship the Lord thy God, and him only shalt thou serve.** Do as Jesus did and quote the Word of God to yourself and your adversary.

Control equals idolatry.

When a person who is controlled becomes *secure only* in a relationship with his or her controller, it amounts to a form of idolatry. Because both individuals in that relationship look to each other as their security, they become one another's god. That is idolatry!

Matthew 4:10, which we have just mentioned, is just one scripture that will sever this kind of control.

If you are under the abusive control of another individual, you need to deal with that situation, because both you and your controller are miserable anyway. Why not get things right with God? To do this, you will have to learn to pray and break the power of the controlling spirit — and all the spirits that go with it, such as fear, guilt, obligation, confusion, and frustration.

When you break the grip of control over your life, it doesn't mean that you won't experience a certain degree of *loneliness*. Those controlling spirits will storm out of your life, and you will be left sitting all alone.

The first thing that will strike you is a feeling of *guilt*, followed by *fear* that you are not capable of making it on your own. You will begin to ask yourself, "What am I going to do now?"

Don't panic. And don't give up. Stop in your tracks and say, "Devil, move, in Jesus' name! I break your power over me. Get off of me. You are a liar!'' Keep using your authority to rebuke guilt and fear, in the name of Jesus. (1 Tim. 2:7.)

Realize that control is not just a natural psychological problem; it is also a *spiritual* problem. As we noted earlier, human nature is naturally controlling. But when control becomes unnatural, it is demonic, and you must fight it — every day.

It doesn't matter whether you feel that you are no longer under guilt or fear, you still must be on your guard. When you get up in the morning, make sure that the first thing you do is to tell those controlling spirits to leave you alone. Break their power over you. Command them to go from you, in Jesus' name. Quote scriptures to them and make them obey you.

The next time you meet the controller, he or she may not speak to you because you haven't been in contact or asked for help. But don't dare feel guilty or try to make up. *You have just won your freedom, so enjoy it!*

4. *Confront your controller.*

First comes the initial break from the controlling person. After you are strong in the Spirit, and you know that your heart is right, then you can take the final step in your complete deliverance from control: confronting your controller!

The Battle of Confrontation

Confrontation does not always have to be a battle. But when confronting a controller, you must be strong, because controllers are not the most logical people to deal with. They have been blinded by their own insecurities.

You must say to your controller, ''You have controlled me in these ways [name them]. I *love* you, but these things will not work in my life anymore. You must change or we can no longer have a relationship.''

When you do this, several things are likely to happen. As soon as you accuse the other person of controlling you, he or she will probably protest, "I'm not trying to control you. I love you. Everything I have done has been for your benefit. Do you mean to tell me that you don't appreciate it?''

Or, the controller will turn the tables on you and try to hide his or her mistakes and wrongs by making it appear that everything that has happened has been your fault.

If you are not strong, you will slip from your stand in the *Spirit* into the *soulish* realm, which is an emotional realm. The controller will continue, "You know I love you; we just have to work this out.'' You will burst into tears and say, "Oh, I know.'' Then you will be back in the clutches of control again!

The controller will manifest all sorts of strong emotions: anger, jealousy, pride, fear, and many others. No normal human being could change emotions so quickly; this is further evidence of the controlling spirits at work within that individual. If you are really strong in the Lord, you can watch and call the name of each spirit as it is manifested.

Know this: You are in a war, not on a vacation. If you are weak, you had better call in a team of strong prayer warriors to back you in intercession as you enter this battle.

After the confrontation is over, don't sit and meditate about what has happened. Don't think about it at all! Shut it out of your mind. Instead of dwelling on it and rehashing it over and over again, get up and walk around the room, praying as you go.

The Price

There are always those who are not willing to pay the price to go on with the Lord. They would rather stay in their own little rut and not have to be concerned with change.

If you truly desire to go on with God, then you may well have to pay this price: You may have to make the very difficult decision to turn loose of friends or other close associates who do not choose to go on and who will oppose your doing so.

You will continue to love them, pray for them, communicate with them, and even visit them; however, with love and firmness, you will not allow them to hinder you or dissuade you from doing what you have to do to fulfill your godly call and purpose.

Do not bow to or serve the insecurities in another person. Do not allow fear to abort your destiny, your mission for God in the earth. Be bold and be strong: walk in the compassion of God and take the nations in His name!

13
Prayer for Freedom

Father, we thank You for this message on control. We thank You for the understanding that You are giving us and the wisdom to discern accurately the difference between hindrances and blessings in our lives. We give You the glory for it.

I thank You, Father, that You want to see people set free from the power of abusive control. I send the Word of God to them now, and I break the power of controlling spirits over them: Satan, let the people go free, in Jesus' name!

I break the power of fear. I tear down the negative, soulish words that have been spoken over people, and I call for clarity and direction to come to them so they can fulfill the plan of God.

I thank You, Lord, that You are giving the people revelation concerning their circumstances, so they can know what to do to be set free.

Father, I thank You that not one person feels that we are against him or her.

Thank You, Father, for the strong leadership You are causing to come forth now through the Body of Christ. We ask You for the boldness to be witnesses of the Gospel in greater power and manifestation. The purpose of God shall be fulfilled in the earth!

Let the Word begin to divide the truth from the false, and bring forth freedom in people's lives, so that their homes may be filled with the presence, power, and joy of the Lord.

In Jesus' name, we thank You for these things and expect to receive them. Amen!

Roberts Liardon was born in Tulsa, Oklahoma. He was born again, baptized in the Holy Spirit, and called to the ministry at the age of eight, after being caught up to Heaven by the Lord Jesus.

Roberts was powerfully commissioned by the Lord to study the lives of God's great "generals" — men and women of faith who were mightily used by God in the past — in order to learn why they succeeded and why they failed.

At age fourteen, Roberts began preaching and teaching in various churches — denominational and non-denominational alike — Bible colleges and universities. He has traveled extensively in the United States and Canada, and his missions outreaches have taken him to Africa, Europe and Asia. Many of his books have been translated into foreign languages.

Roberts preaches and ministers under a powerful anointing of the Holy Spirit. In his sermons, Roberts calls people of all ages to salvation, holiness and life in the Holy Spirit.

Through Roberts' ministry around the world, many people have accepted God's call to yield themselves as vessels for the work of the Kingdom.

To contact the author,
write:

Roberts Liardon
P. O. Box 23238
Minneapolis, Minnesota 55423

*Please include your prayer requests
and comments when you write.*

Other Books by Roberts Liardon

Kathryn Kuhlman
A Spiritual Biography
of God's Miracle Working Power

Spiritual Timing

Run to the Battle

Learning To Say No Without Feeling Guilty

I Saw Heaven

Success in Life and Ministry

The Quest for Spiritual Hunger

The Price of Spiritual Power

The Invading Force

Religious Politics

Cry of the Spirit

Videos by Roberts Liardon

The Lord Is a Warrior

I Saw Heaven

Stirring Up the Gifts of God

God's Generals
(8-volume set of tapes, 60 minutes each)

**Available from your local bookstore
or by writing:**

Harrison House
P. O. Box 35035 • Tulsa, OK 74153

In Canada contact:

Word Alive • P. O. Box 284
Niverville, Manitoba • CANADA ROA 1EO

For international sales in Europe, contact:

Harrison House Europe • Belruptstrasse 42 A
A — 6900 Bregenz • AUSTRIA

The Harrison House Vision

Proclaiming the truth and the power
Of the Gospel of Jesus Christ
With excellence;

Challenging Christians to
Live victoriously,
Grow spiritually,
Know God intimately.